One

OF THE MANY

Roses

A Book of Poetry
By Gary E. McCormick

Dedication

For Jean
My children and grandchildren
For those who follow
Look for the gratitude in these words

One of the Many Roses

A Book of Poetry by Gary E. McCormick

Acknowledgments

Many thanks for the following publications
in which many of my poems have appeared:

The Other Side of the Lake
The Chicago Tribune Sunday Magazine
Peninsula Poets
Denver Post Poetry Forum
Green's Magazine
Hartford Courant
Oregonian Verse

Cover and book design by Chris Robinson
Production and typesetting by Circle Associates
Published by GEM Press
Printed by Batson Printing, Inc. • Benton Harbor, Michigan

ISBN   0-9630037-0-4

Contents

One of the Many Roses

You stand out
  with your flaws
in the montage
  of glorious tints
shades and tones
  of every color

Your subtle hue
  tinged with a
stain distinguishes
  a kind of survival

Brilliance is your
  vivid strength

You are special
  in a wild variety

One of the many

Singing With Candles
A Memorial To The Vietnam Dead, 1968

They sang with candles
When he was one;
Twenty-one.

A birthday card
Delivered on his
Deathday.

In a tomb
On his anniversary
From the womb.

We lost four-hundred-four.
They: seven-hundred-two,
Today.

We lost less,   a lot less:
Won the war of numbing numbers,
Today.

They will sing
with candles, not knowing,
Tomorrow.

There will be less,   a lot less,
Singing with candles,
Tomorrow.

Relief

A breeze slipped in,
catching and cooling the feet
that felt the firey floor of the steel mill,
that carried the weight of the working man,
who walked ten hours today for wages:
   for the right to return home,
   to take off his shoes and socks,
   to sit back and bide some time
   waiting for a breeze to slip in.

Cement and Powder

Cement chafed hands,
Made rough from mortar,
Wipe the brow, wet from
Working all day with brick,
Wrinkled from a back breaking
Callous making forty hour week.

Satin soft Suzanne, the pretty powder puff,
Waits to be lightly touched and
Loved by her mason man;
The gentle man with hardened hands,
Tender hands.

Near the Tip of the Big Dipper

It free falls in a streak:
A cosmic slash of silver speed
That's lost in a flash like
A quick brilliant thought.

First Litter

Suckling kittens,
Six blind tiger-mice,
Plush bundles of purr,
Siphon milk with
Monotone tunes
Of sugar hums
And honey solos.
So soft is the
Simmer of their
Sweet singing.

The Year the Robin Came Too Soon

The blizzard zeroes through the orchard
As buds clamp their half-open eyes dead shut.
Orange breast feathers are decoupaged
Under icy lacquer on a powder gray barn side.

A young lady in Daytona Beach
Applies cocoa butter to burnt skin
Dreams of sweet hollow chocolate Easter bunnies
As a splash of ocean spray slides a cold drop
Down the well-done shell of her chilly spine.

The Night of the Storm

The storm comes
Smashing snares
Crashing cymbals
On and on and on
Downpour pounds
Thunder drones
Down down down
Sheets on sheets
Rush and roar

The wind screams
Through the woods
End over end over end

The early morning sun
Comes up golden
Shines on a cat's whisker
Comes up silver
Sings in a bird's whistle

Lilacs

I'm
seldom stunned

But this morning
the dewborne scent
of fresh morning lilacs
sent me staggering in a daze

Indeed,
it was a shock
of windblown power
so fragrant, so potent

It leveled me
with a sweet purple jolt

Winter Vision

The fine snow falls
Like the last breath
Of a soft whisper
As it changes its name
On the lips of a slow stream.

It comes very quickly
This winter vision
In the wink of a swift instant
On this will-o'-the-wisp evening.

Birch Bark Canoe

They piece it together
With careful seaworthy artistry:
Thwarts, inwales, outwales, gunwales,
Lash it with split roots of black spruce;
Apply Indian gum pitch, bark,
Dry cedar shavings and porcupine quills.

So lightly its launched;
Drifts gently in the yawning hammock,
Yaws softly, streaming along
Wallowing in the hush of rare river silk.

Putting Out Bad Airs

Chimneys sneeze and cough
   clouds of congestion
as the lungs of a big city wheeze.

A freight train clears its throat
   and chugs out of town
with a flatcar of foul air.

The Milky Way
   gropes behind the haze,
squinting through watery eyes.

Spectator of Speed

Strolling, I see first a speck
then a distant charging dot
A mach-quicksilver shot
banshees over my head
rifles into the distance
a dissolving dot
a speck.

My pace decelerates
and so does my pulse
I seem an inchworm
creeping and shrinking

Slowly step by step
I search for specks

Postmark: Port-of-Spain, Trinidad

A sailor near the Equator
watches the ice melt in a double shot of scotch
multiplies emptiness with a stack of chewed swizzle sticks

A lonely lady in Ishpeming
reads a sun burnt letter and chases her chills
divides solace with ninety proof forget-me-not swallows

Today loneliness staggers from place to place
hunts for another spot to hang a good one on
falls flat on its face in a cold empty gutter

Tomorrow it'll be carried out feet first
dead and drowned in a hungover world
looking bloodshot on a stiff stretcher

Someday it might push the rock aside
rise up with keen dry eyes turn it over
ascend into the warm arms of a lover

Early Morning

Your first tear
Is a small dew
Of sorrow.

Your sigh
a first chirp
Of sadness.

Have a good cry
Little girl.

Cry with the birds
Singing on the silver grass
Of early morning.

Blizzard

As I walk out a winter sky slides above
  and an evening chill skates on my cheeks
A flash of freeze slaps me flush on the face
  as I slip into the first rush of flurries
My sight is snow as blinded I bend into
  and slash through the cutting swirling storm
It's a wild whiteout with me shivering within

Lake Daybreak

The first crack in early morning silence
Is the crash of a big one bellysmacking the blue
Sending it swirling into rings of growing rings
The swift keeper darts into the thin shine of daybreak
Sucks in a minnow and dives out of sight
Golden spirals swim closer and closer
Circle slowly slowly out of sight.

The angler drinks in a deep breath of morning
Swings out the line sending a soft spinning
Cane pole now-I'm-gonna-getcha signal.

The moon swings behind the orange morning haze.

The Family Tree

Ancestors are yesterday people
  the lifeless who live yet today
The well known who wrote
  lasting legacies in books of history
The little known who left only
  lingering memories in minds of kinsfolk

Ancestors are those buried
  who left a breath and spirit
six feet above shoveled earth

Thoughts in a Maternity Ward

A stubborn chunk of chalk
 harbors in tree shade
as a crocus grunts forth
 birthing headfirst to daylight

In this context I watch
 your pink wrinkles blossom
your blue eyes bloom
 born this blessed spring day

Rain Traffic

Looking through window raindrops
  is like looking sideways into the sea
no fish   only vehicles swimming
  some surfacing   some submerging

The school of traffic is a sea jam
  wandering semis're whales
shifty sports car's a seahorse
  cabs're crawling yellow crabs
dolphins ride back to back

The waterbug skitters
  through window raindrops.

Withdrawal Philosophy

The under-the-Christmas-tree kids
Halloween-trick-or-treat kids
Easter-egg-hunt kids
Have closed their minds

The Baptism kids
First Holy Communion kids
Confirmation kids
No longer believe

The rock-me-to-sleep kids
Kiss-me-goodnight kids
Let-me-sit-on-your-lap kids
Have turned their backs

With a no-birthday-candle wish
God-is-dead, no-bedtime-story philosophy
They have withdrawn from the establishment

I think of this as I place a secure comforter
Around my small conformer   who sleeps
Tooth beneath pillow   dreaming silver coins

Peptic Kin

This well-to-do executive charged
   with the business
Of many major industries
   works long hard hours
Investing in a set of ulcers.

A ne'er-do-well hobo content
   with riding the rails
Travels the country
   many long tedious miles
Earning a set of ulcers.

They're brothers of the ulcer,
   peptic kin.
Big difference is:
   one can afford soothing medicine
The other rides on and on
   with an awful grinding pain
Gnawing at his gut.

One of the Three

Yes,
I met a wise man
Dressed like a Mercedes
Bearing a rich Aramco aroma

I'll bet
He's the one
Who brought the myrrh

But his motives
Were questionable
'Cause the swaddled babe
Didn't want to make a fuss

A low profile incarnate

Drifting Day Into Night

White on white
   speckled under wild dogwood blooms
trilliums spot the ravine
   like dots of cotton spatter furrows
of a southern fried field.

Stars reach down
   peck the river
like bugs of lightning
   spark dark corners
of a night of northern lights.

My canoe drifts softly
   I drink in the day and night
my thirst is quenched by
   trilliums and stars
dogwood blooms and moonbeams.

Sundown in G Major

The overture marches off the
   bank's wintergreen dome
As the crowd strides a cadence
   toward the band shell
On the bluff.

Howard's redcoats strike up the band
   as the sun shimmies over the oboes
Sinks low over the cymbals
   puts carats in the gleam
Of shining brass.

The orange ball dances in the gold
   glides with ballet grace
Slides slowly down
   to the soft slow roll
Of humming timpani.

Sails tack into the rainbow glow
   mallards ride the flow
Woodwinds gershwin a score
   to the train's marching rattle
Of shaking tambourines.

The bluff is alive
   with the crescendo chorus
Of staccato applause
   as the redcoats rise
and a melodious ovation stands.

North Pier Dawn

It's a keen and easy morning
When the geese sweep out of the east
Design a distant symmetry of shape
Arrow into a rare high geometry
Narrow low into a fine line
To be swallowed by a white sky.

The St. Joe river swims quickly
Toward the great lake as a golden
Sunrise nips at its white-capped heels.

Afterbirth

A strong heartbeat
pulses in a bead of sweat
that breaks slow from her brow.

It splatters on the floor
scatters like mercury splits
seeking the heart of its center.

Her labor ends in a cry
screaming a last spasm
shrieking a release of life.

She died in the afterbirth
wet sweat and bloody aftermath
of breeding the first heartbeat
in her sweet bloodwet screamer.

Magnum Solution

Bang is a
Blasting cannon
Blowing brains away.

A short
Soggy note
Spells a red
Wet conclusion.

It says
Something about
Giving up
Not wanting to live.

It ends with goodbye
And the finger that
Pressed the pencil
Pulled the trigger.

To Babes So New

The pink wrinkled fists
Can't know to whom
They'll be raised in anger
What excitement will
Bring them down
Upon tables of joy
With whom they'll carry
On in close embrace
Or when they'll unfold
To tenderness of love's touch.

There are those who
Now fold their hands
Pray only for gentleness
To free flow in the fresh
Wrinkles of pink tender fists.

A Matter of Timing

Death   just a beat away
A clock full of essential tocks and ticks
Tick   tock   toward the last sigh
Waits for the tired spring to unwind
Stops dead   right on time
Absolutely split second timing takes us

Flat Out

I'm hellbent for the horizon
Footflooring a highballing rig
Reeling in a sleek yellow streak
From a clear rear mirror.

The blacktop unwinds
Like a sheet of fast tarpaper
Abandon swirls in the slipstream
As a reckless wind snaps at my ass.

I let'er rip over the rim
Spurting a loud sputtering trail
Of roaring loose bowels as a
Ten-ton cat stare banshees by
Slamming me with a sideswipe slap.

We're sixteen wheel night riders
Growling the quiet out of a peaceful eve.

Other Lifetimes

When I was a bird,
a Cliff Swallow
 soaring about the bluffs
sometime back
       so many
long lifetimes ago,
I praised every sailing
slow motion sweep
       I swept from
bluff to bluff and back
the Lake Michigan wind
whipping my tailfeathers
       clipping me
with cuffs of windbursts
playing my wingtips aloft
sending me drifting
       toward home
to the sand hole perch
tucked above the beach

Yes, I had many lifetimes
 and I chose to be man most often
because brilliant intellect
intrigued me immensely
       and it's during
these intellectual flits
of high poetic flight
that I reminisce
most about my
swallow ways and eagle days
it's then I wish for the wind
will to be on the wing again
       the next time out

Autumn Stains

Bursts of canary
russet and berry
explode in the dust
of a glorious Autumn dawn
staining the leaves and fields
of Fall.

A ringneck becomes
its camouflage
clucking in a cover
of pheasant color
blending with the leaves and fields
of Fall.

Arrowheads of geese
shoot southward
dissolving in cotton trails
puffs on the line drawn horizon
painted above the leaves and fields
of Fall.

Brush Strokes

He touches the shadow
　of each eye with his lips
steps back blows a kiss
　brushes her heart
with sure soft strokes

Her reaction is mesmerized
　in the vivid oils
of the brilliant canvas

The smile is enigmatic
　eyes inviting heart static

After Dinner

The sherbet's
cool and sweet
orange buds
break icy
over goosebumps
on my tongue

And now
for the green heat
of that smooth
mint spirit

Behind the Bar

It's the first one
   that multiples
like a mirror full
   of bottles

Count the labels
   one by deadly one
They add up to death
   one shot at a time

Stare in a stupor
   that's you   you
glassy eyed boozer
   reflect on it

Storyboard

Ballyhoo
bright stuff
neon adjectives
glittering superlatives
animated redundancies
brilliant boobtube bullshit

The Deep Six-Feet Down Blues

They sway
   singing deep down
purple feeling blues
   wailing and reeling
moaning swooning

They're singing
   for Satchmo's
silent brass

How do you like
   those low down
eulogy blues, Louie?

Formula of the Heart

How do you compute
love's mathematics?

Is it
this plus that
equals our love?

Or is what's left
abstract subtraction?

Can we divide it into
minute lasting amounts?

Multiplication
magnifies it.

Place the calculator
in the pocket
over your heart
gently.

Heartbeats
humming computations
harmonize.

1976, Buy(Ten Cent)ial in Retrospect

Do your remember
the influx of flags?

Recall the red white blue betsy american ross kind
thirteen and fifty star banners spangled from bumpers
furled free or cheap to citizens for boxtops and coupons

We gloried for those
independence hucksters:
selling polyester drip dry genuine
pledge allegiance antique war torn
two-hundred-year old Taiwan old glories

Oh Oh say can
you see those stars and bars
hailing proudly glaring redly bursting bombly
waving grandly from frisbees and six pack throwaways

Do you remember
sweeping away the star studded litter
bagging the bicentennial trash
when the parade ended when the last
firework fluttered into the dumpster

Disco Din

Pulses quick and dizzy
blaze in dazing exertion

Shock waves sock out
blasting a stereo blare
dancers twist and shout
loud screams for more
are whispers in a roar

A singer mimics to the mike
I read lusty lyrics on her lips

Lights pulse brightly
keep time   keep dizzy pulsing time

My circuit breaker pops

Cliche

"You're pretty as a picture."
Nothing hackneyed about that.

She was plain, never heard
such words before in her context.

What she heard was as fresh
as the rose tucked beneath
the pillow of her beautiful dream.

Hardening of an Essential Artery

I think it'll be white
but it's colorless
Feels like seeing
Yet I'm breathlessly
blind

a sigh inside me
swims slowly to the rim
Darkness screws the lid down
drowns me deeply tightly
with a torque wrench
wrist

my heart is smothered
under a shovel full of sea
Whole graveyards sink
ghostlike into the dusty
deep

I am submerged
interred still   mourned

Full Moon, Silver Night

Snow
shining white
still and soft
shows the silhouette shadows
of the willow's slim fingers
under this full silver moon

The bough is black, limbs are lace
delicately shadow dancing in the light
of the full moon of shining silver.

Dialogue

So this Grackle flies up and asks:
"Where can a bird like me get a breath of fresh air?"
And a smart aleck flower follows up with this statement:
"When you stop doing your thing on everything!"
With that, black wings flutter dropping a
Smelly shot of white paste in the black eye
Of a surprised Susan dancing in a field of sisters.

A Chancy Life

He must have been close to 76,
this man of gray, wrinkles and wisdom.
He spoke from the pulpit without a collar
admitting his faults to others like himself.

They listened nodding their "we've been theres."
He said he got his second chance one day after he was born
and his latest chance sometime early that very morning.

He laughed about his more than twenty seven thousand chances
and so did the crowd of laughing day-at-a-time chance takers.

Red Wings on Fence Posts

Measured in nearly exact increments
the black birds preen their wings
and sing spring to the roaring expressway,
a biker on a country road hears the crisp,
clear chortle calls of these early arrivals.

A Speechwriter Makes a Point: Rhetoric Comes to Light

Kinder and gentler
That's what he says
he says it a lot so
he must mean it and
the press says he says it
so it must mean what it says
when it's said so often

A nun in the soup kitchen
pours a kind bowl of love
and gets a gentle nod of thanks

An addict kinda hears the quote
as a gent pushes him into hell

So they still say it
again and again and again
kinder gentler kinder gentler
some do it   some say it   some be it.

A bulb flashes above the
guy on the word processor who
begins a beam countdown to make points.

Skull Place

The carpenter's son
helps us make some sense
of that hill of bones
occupied by those who
die day after day innocent
forgiving the guy on the
cross next door buried deep
in our daily place of skulls.

Despite all the Advice

Mom said
say please and thank you
Dad demanded
keep your nose clean
Nuns pleaded
pray to your guardian angel
Coaches yelled
keep your head down, your guard up
Friends pointed out
pitfalls and possible pratfalls
They all tried to help
with their two cents worth
of do it my way not your way
I remember this as I prepare
some good advice for my children

Garden Thoughts

Every shovel dig
turns loose that
fresh black aroma

Even rubbing it
between your fingers
releases the sharp smell
of new growth
like breaking beads popping
free a deep earth smell
essential to the soft
fragrance of wild
strawberries in bloom

From a Bus Window

Scenes rush by
Swiftly so swiftly

   Redwings bending branches
   Doves flitting darting
   Swallows diving dancing
   Dead fur squashed flat
   Crows dodging to the shoulder

Scenes rush by
Swiftly so swiftly

   Wheat barely green
   Fields plowed black
   Polka dot bandanas flash
   Planters bent tractoring
   Furrows row on row meander

Scenes rush by
Swiftly so swiftly

Bleached barns bend
Sole chimneys stand
Skeleton outhouses lean
Grey shredded curtains sway
Busted orange flower pots pose

Scenes rush by
Swiftly so swiftly

School yards ablaze
Children ablast swings pumping
Tagging racing jumping
Teachers waving shouting
Teeter totter monkey bars bustling

Scenes rush by
Swiftly so swiftly

The rubber humming bus swallows
yellow dashes all the way to New Orleans
as the wiper sweeps the swift rushing scenery

Swift scenes
Rush swiftly by

The British Have a Way of Putting It

The BBC broadcaster says the plane
costs 3 hundred thousand million dollars.
Seems so much more than the mere billions
Brokaw bellyaches about it in a little snippet
before sign off and that 30 second spot selling bras.

Just the Fax, Hon!

We met fax to fax
On a legal sized sheet.
Her vitals were blurred
In the wrinkles of a flimsy copy.

But we persevere faxing.
Her in Palm Springs, me in Berrien Springs.
Our first date cost seven bucks and pennies,

A modem romance and we cherish the receipt
As we dance check to check over phone lines.

Crude

The hiker puts his canteen
under the fresh spray of the waterfall
lifts the ice cool metal to his lips
and swallows in deep quenching gulps,
quickly he hunches over in cramped spasms
as the slippery black fluid oozes in painful
vomit from his choking, coughing throat.

Slick sea otters of Prince William Sound
hungrily circle the hull of the Exxon Valdez.

Crisp Alaskan air spills pure over its creaking deck
as geese dip down into the crystal chill of the bay.

A man sleeps   intoxicated by it all.

Jazz Piano

All eighty eight of 'em
Tickling teasing tapping
Tempo rhythm melody
Syncopating dissonant
Soft slow pervasive
Symmetric sharp swirling
Ten fingers swinging reckless
Loud   clanging jamming
Percolating gliding brewing
Humming jumping jiving
All black and white of 'em

St. Joe Questions

What's so special about
  the city on the bluff?
Are the answers blended
  in the magnificent alchemy
Of a rosy will-o'-the-wisp sunset?

The watchers on the bluff
  ponder the questions
As the gleaming great lake
  swallows the sinking sun.

This twilight the answers
  are glorious in the rosy glow.

Big Band Blast

The piano softly points the direction
    before the brass declare the pace
and set the screaming spirit of the flying
    hot swing of the fast jamming jazz band.

Solos smoothly come and go, styling the mood
    from sax to sax, trumpet to trumpet, bone to bone.
The ivories wax eloquently to the beat
    of the snapping snare and breezy cymbals.

The counterpoint blend of bass and eighty-eights
    announce the fusion of a cool conclusion.

The Other Side

His gut drops on the elevator floor
   as it sucks the air out of his lungs
On its way to the tip of the Sears Tower.

There he aims his high powered telescope
   across the great lake and spies a blonde
Invisibly splashing her bikini in the sand.

Their first sight is love as their eyes
   meet in the flash of a reflected lens
They blow kisses from high rises and beaches
   across whitecaps to lovers on the other side.

Thoughts About China

What you do can be very dangerous
say the elders to the young as they
head to their tea party in the square
as they march toward the lady of liberty
standing proud above the crowd of young
freedom lovers ready to fight for the promises
made by the leaders who hide behind soldier rifles.

The elders warn them and wish them well
some join them as they stand firm in front of tanks.

The nightly news puts the finger on martyrs who
will feel cold steel at the base of their skull.

The bloody explosion racks the hearts of the world

Lake Michigan Sunset

The bright orange ball of sun
cut in half by the horizon
ducks deep beneath the great lake
 holds its breath and swims slowly
surfaces at daybreak behind the loungers
 sitting in the sunwatch bleachers
high on the lake's great bluffs.

They are wonderstruck lovers
 of the rising and setting sun.

The Creative Team

They design the butterfly
for the top left hand corner
of the bold corporate logo.

It's willowy with wings
mellow lacey delicate subtle
monarchically black and yellow.

It looks best on the corner
of an upper case character
beginning the proud name of a
producer of litter for mass market
landfills overflowing with its excess success.

The butterfly designer scowls.

Stop Sign

The white throws
its hands up warning
out of the bright red
It yells halt
with a red white
   whoa

Brakes grab grip
tires bite slide
as eighteen wheels
skid and screech to a
   standstill

Ugly Birds

You know who I mean
   those purple black ones
with glossy purple heads
   sometimes brown crowns or
just shiny jet black domes.

They call them various names
   cowbirds starlings grackles.

Don't you feel grackle sounds
   more like the way
those ugly black on black
   ichabod-crane-like birds look?

Another Prayer

Stretching into the blue
   the Heron swims through the wind

Grateful for the sight
   the watcher silently says so

Somewhere someone composes
   an all encompassing supplication

The rainbow simply says thanks

Prestidigitation

Now you see them now you don't
gone in a flurry of blurred wings
the hummingbirds enchant majestically
invisible in their impetuous suspension
vanish radiate dissolve illuminate

Presto   the magician smiles at his
wild fluttering   ruby throated   sleight of hand

Fingerpainting

He daubs a little here
dabs a little there
strokes colors rubs

Blue bleeds blue
red washes red
white blends white

He swirls majestically
sun cloud sky
green landscape brown

The stick people
show tall and proud
on the preschool wall

The master smiles
and circles a
happy face family

How to Please a Goblin

They come to my door
  bags open begging
teeth flashing scaring
  jack-o'-lanterns
howling house to house

I feed peanutbutter cups
  to my ghoulish phantoms
who smile masked sweet smiles
  then slink giggling
          into the Halloween night

Awesome

This day in August
  is right for watercolors and oils
with the water crisp and clear
  the sky blue on blue on blue
only soft cumulus brushstrokes

We sit in the warm dunes
  watching miraculous Monarchs
come off the wrinkled lake
  their paper thin beauty
masking their strenuous flight

Indefatigable they soar
  high up and over
the swallow-marked bluffs
  undaunted and dogged
they flutter out of sight

It Was Said With Such Authority

I'll give you the gist of
  what was said

It was about love
  and the sayer
said it had nothing to do
  with receiving

He said
  love was all about giving
plain and simple

You could tell this guy
  walked the talk

He made it clear
  you must love yourself
before you can
  begin to love another

The guy reminded me
  of that lover from Galilee

Calculations

Enter any number
  press the times sign
and multiply it
  with another number

see the total on display
  it comes nowhere near
expressing the feelings
  I have for you

the liquid crystal
  sums up our love

Begging at the Birdfeeder

Scruffy
feathers all out of whack
chitters incessantly
for anything to quiet
a low hungry growl
skips about non stop
scatters a feeder of seeds
waits impatiently for a handout

Mom
gives in
deposits a seed
in a chattering bill

She
sings a
learn to do it yourself
scolding type of twitter